INFORMATION
EXPLORER
JUNIOR

Find Your Way with Atlases

by Adrienne Matteson

CHERRY LAKE PUBLISHING · ANN ARBOR, MICHIGAN

CHERRY
LAKE
Publishing

A NOTE TO PARENTS AND TEACHERS: Please remind your children how to stay safe online before they do the activities in this book.

A NOTE TO KIDS: Always remember your safety comes first!

Published in the United States of America
by Cherry Lake Publishing
Ann Arbor, Michigan
www.cherrylakepublishing.com

Content Adviser: Gail Dickinson, PhD, Associate Professor, Old Dominion University

Book design and illustration: The Design Lab

Photo credits: Cover, ©iStockphoto.com/zorani; page 6, ©Photowitch/Dreamstime.com; page 7, ©iStockphoto.com/skynesher; page 16, ©iStockphoto.com/gbh007; page 17, ©William Silver/Shutterstock, Inc.; page 18, ©EastVillage Images/Shutterstock, Inc.; page 20, ©javarman/Shutterstock, Inc.

Library of Congress Cataloging-in-Publication Data
Matteson, Adrienne.
  Find your way with atlases / by Adrienne Matteson.
    p. cm. — (Information explorer junior)
  Includes bibliographical references and index.
  ISBN 978-1-61080-370-0 (lib. bdg.)—ISBN 978-1-61080-379-3 (e-book)—
ISBN 978-1-61080-395-3 (pbk.)
1. Atlases—Juvenile literature. I. Title.
  G1021.M2574 2012
  912—dc23   2011034965

Cherry Lake Publishing would like to acknowledge
the work of The Partnership for 21st Century Skills.
Please visit www.21stcenturyskills.org for more information.

Printed in the United States of America
Corporate Graphics Inc.
January 2012
CLSP10

Table of Contents

CHAPTER ONE

What Is an Atlas?

Have you ever wondered how many states touch the Mississippi River? Or where the tallest mountain in the world is? Or if there *really* is a Timbuktu?

Where in the world is Timbuktu?

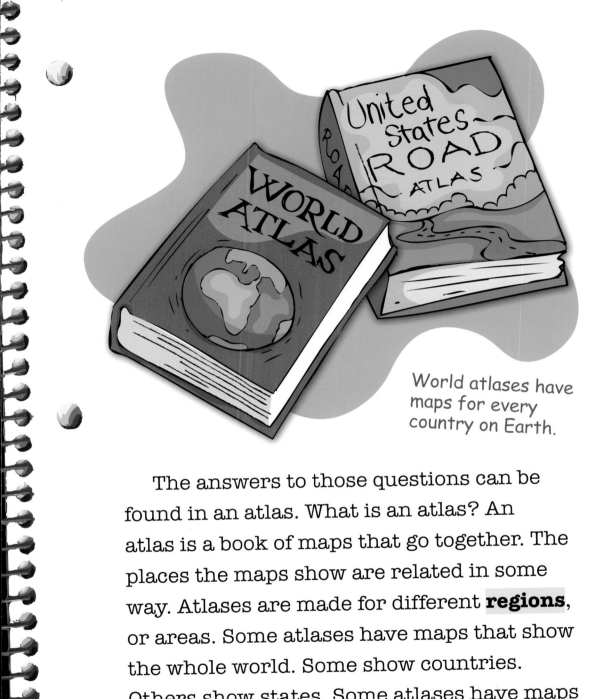

World atlases have maps for every country on Earth.

The answers to those questions can be found in an atlas. What is an atlas? An atlas is a book of maps that go together. The places the maps show are related in some way. Atlases are made for different **regions**, or areas. Some atlases have maps that show the whole world. Some show countries. Others show states. Some atlases have maps that show all of these things.

Atlases can teach you a lot about places you've never been.

Maps can tell us many things about a country or a state. Some of these things include:

- Where the rivers, lakes, and mountains are
- Where its **borders** are
- What the capital city is
- How many people live there
- Where the famous places are
- What kind of **crops** are grown there
- The history of the place

The most common atlas is a world atlas. That's a book of maps that covers all of the cities and countries in the world. But there are also

other kinds of atlases. A **historical** atlas
tells you about how an area was in the past.
A road atlas shows you all of the roads and
highways you should take on your family
vacation.

Each map in an atlas might tell us about
one place within a bigger area. Or it might
include information on different topics about
the area. Put together, these maps tell us the
story of that area and its people.

Maps can show you how to get where you need to go.

Open a world atlas to the pages showing the United States of America. You will probably find at least two maps for the country. One is a **political map**. The other is a **physical map**.

A political map shows borders and the names of places.

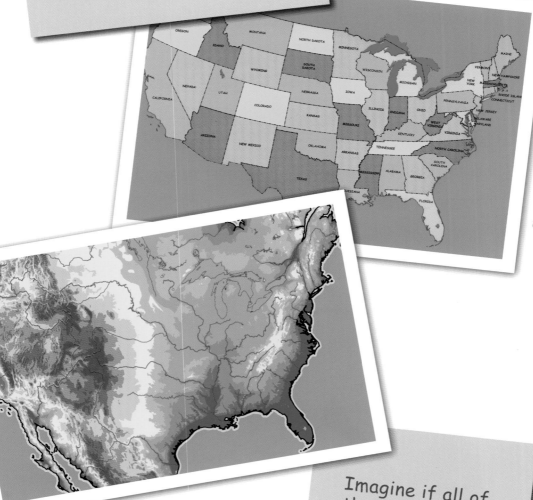

A physical map shows the physical features of the land, such as rivers, mountains, and lakes.

Imagine if all of that information were on the same map. It would be really confusing!

To get a copy of this activity, visit www.cherrylakepublishing.com/activities.

Activity

Political and physical maps use colors differently. The map's colors tell you what kind of map it is. Take a look at some maps in a world atlas. Can you tell which ones are political maps? Can you tell which ones are physical maps? Here's a helpful hint. The states or countries on a political map have different colors so you can see the borders. Physical maps use greens and browns to show how high the land is.

Political maps show which land belongs to which countries.

9

CHAPTER TWO

Tools to Unlock Your Atlas

Map keys can be different for each map.

A lot of important information needs to fit onto a map. So mapmakers often use colors and symbols instead of words. Each page in an atlas has a small box called the **map key**. Sometimes it's called the legend. The map key tells us what each symbol and color means. Sometimes reading a map can be like cracking a code. Reading the key helps you break that code.

There is also an atlas key at the beginning of the book. It will tell you the following:

- What kinds of lines are used for state and country borders
- What shapes and symbols are used to show cities (sometimes big cities are marked with a different symbol than small cities)
- What the colors mean on both physical and political maps

Stars are often used to show where capital cities are located.

Take a look at the key and the scale if you ever get confused.

This information will be true for all of the maps in the atlas. Think you might forget what a symbol or a color means? You can always go back to the atlas key to check!

Other things to look for in the map key are the **scale** and the **compass rose**.

A scale tells us how much real land the map represents. A map of the world and a map of your neighborhood can be the same size on paper. But the real land that your neighborhood takes up is much smaller. For example, 1 inch (2.54 centimeters) on a world map could be equal to 1,000 miles (1,609 kilometers). But 1 inch on your neighborhood map may equal only 1 mile (1.6 km).

The compass rose looks like a pointy cross. It tells us where north, south, east, and west are on the map. North is usually up. Look carefully, though. North is not always up!

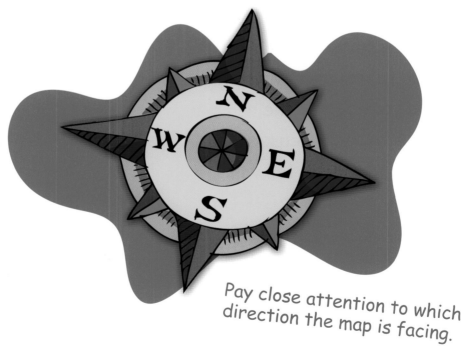

Pay close attention to which direction the map is facing.

Activity

Look at a map of the United States. Use a ruler to measure how many inches New York City, New York, is from Los Angeles, California. Then check the map scale to see how many miles each inch represents. Multiply that number by the number of inches you measured. The answer will tell you how many miles it is from New York City to Los Angeles!

To get a copy of this activity, visit www.cherrylakepublishing.com/activities.

Now look at your map of the United States again. Find out how many miles it is between:

- Houston, Texas, and Washington, D.C.
- Miami, Florida, and Seattle, Washington
- Phoenix, Arizona, and Cincinnati, Ohio
- Dallas, Texas, and Minneapolis, Minnesota

CHAPTER THREE

Grids and the Gazetteer

Let's say you know the name of a place. But you don't know where to find it in the atlas. You can look up place names in the **gazetteer**. That is the **index** of the atlas.

Use the gazetteer whenever you need to find a specific map.

Yosemite National Park is a fun place to visit.

The gazetteer is a list of all of the places and physical features named on the maps in your atlas. It's like a book index. A gazetteer is in alphabetical order.

Imagine that your teacher has asked you to find Yosemite National Park in your atlas. Go to the gazetteer and look under the letter Y. Then look for "Yosemite National Park."

A good atlas can help you find beautiful sights in Yosemite National Park.

You will see a page number. You'll also see a code made up of a letter and a number. It will look like this:

Yosemite National Park, p.26 F4

Page 26 has a map of California. That is where Yosemite National Park is located. But what does F4 mean? To answer this, look closer at the map. Each map in the atlas has letters going up the sides. There are also

numbers going across the top and bottom.
These letters and numbers make up a **grid**.
This helps you find places on the map.
Yosemite National Park is in the place where
row F meets column 4.

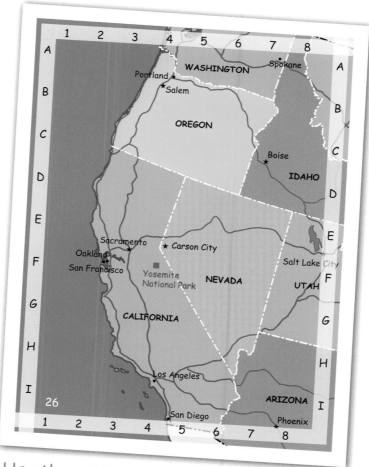

Use the grid to find out exactly where
you need to go.

To get a copy of this activity, visit www.cherrylakepublishing.com/activities.

Activity

Many cities in the world have the same name. Let's find some. Look up the following city names in the gazetteer in your world atlas. Then find each place on a map.

- San José
- Lincoln
- Buenos Aires
- Union

There are many cities named Buenos Aires. The most famous one is in Argentina.

Maps help us see our world in new and exciting ways. You can learn a lot from physical and political maps. Other maps can show you where certain languages are spoken or where the most people live. An atlas is an important tool. It is also a fun one. Enjoy it!

Glossary

borders (BOR-dirz) the dividing lines between countries, states, or regions

compass rose (KUHM-puhss ROZE) a cross-like symbol that shows where north, south, east, and west are on the map

crops (KROPS) plants grown in large amounts, usually for food

gazetteer (gaz-uh-TIHR) the index of an atlas, which lists the names of places, rivers, oceans, and other land features alphabetically

grid (GRID) a frame of crisscrossed rows (across) and columns (down) that help to locate places on a map

historical (hi-STOR-uh-kuhl) having to do with people or events of the past

index (IN-deks) an alphabetical list of all the topics in a book and the page where each can be found

map key (MAP KEY) a small box on a map that tells what each symbol and color used on the map means

physical map (FIZ-uh-kuhl MAP) a map that shows the features of the land, such as rivers and mountains

political map (puh-LI-ti-kuhl MAP) a map that shows borders and the names of places

regions (REE-juhnz) large areas of land, such as a continent

scale (SKALE) a tool that shows how much real land a map in an atlas represents

Find Out More

BOOKS

The Complete Book of Maps & Geography. Greensboro, NC: Carson-Dellosa Publishing, 2009.

Gonzales, Doreen. Are We There Yet? Using Map Scales. Mankato, MN: Capstone Press, 2008.

National Geographic Kids World Atlas. Des Moines, IA: National Geographic Children's Books, 2010.

WEB SITES

Fact Monster: World Atlas & Map Library

www.factmonster.com/atlas

A great site to help you explore the world! Check out country profiles, world flags, and statistics and facts. Read U.S. state and city profiles, and have geography fun with crossword puzzles and quizzes. You can also print out and color hundreds of different maps of the United States.

National Geographic Maps: Tools for Adventure

www.mywonderfulworld.org/toolsforadventure/games/adventure.html

Check out this fun interactive site to learn how to use maps. You can also play map games that let you explore pyramids and the planet Mars, and even go on a hunt for sunken treasure.

Index

About the Author

Adrienne Matteson is a media specialist in Noblesville, Indiana. She loves maps of all kinds, and sometimes, when she has a little free time, she reads a world atlas for fun.